T0197367

GABRIELLE MANFREDI

A Home Built by Battle

Italo Recine: A Memoir

AuthorHouse™
1663 Liberty Drive
Bloomington, IN 47403
www.authorhouse.com
Phone: 1 (800) 839-8640

Published by AuthorHouse 12/07/2017

ISBN: 978-1-5462-2017-6 (sc)
ISBN: 978-1-5462-2018-3 (e)

Library of Congress Control Number: 2017918673

Print information available on the last page.

Any people depicted in stock imagery provided by Thinkstock are models,
and such images are being used for illustrative purposes only.
Certain stock imagery © Thinkstock.

This book is printed on acid-free paper.

Because of the dynamic nature of the Internet, any web addresses or links contained in this book may have changed
since publication and may no longer be valid. The views expressed in this work are solely those of the author and do not
necessarily reflect the views of the publisher, and the publisher hereby disclaims any responsibility for them.

authorHOUSE®

My cousin, Domenico, and I in the center of Ripi, Italy, where we grew up together

Prelude

We got a letter one day. It wasn't unusual that we got one, we tried communicating with my father occasionally, but this was a different type of letter. My mother didn't know how to read and write and neither did I—I was too young. My sister could read a little bit, but not much. We had to get someone to read the letter to us, like we did whenever we got other letters from our father. This one wasn't generic, though. This letter was asking us to come to America. We were all very excited, ya know. We hadn't seen our father in years—hell, I hadn't seen him since I was 9 months old…and to meet him in America of all places? Well, we thought that would change our lives. Of course, this was before the war, though. We didn't foresee the battles we would have to overcome to get to my father in America. We didn't foresee any of them at all.

1.

We were just lying there… in the fields. My friend, Bastiano, and I, we were eight or nine at the time—and we were just lying there in the tall, grassy fields behind my house, staring at the sky. That's when I heard it, a horrible sound. A now, very familiar sound…that meant planes were coming. And then I saw it. It came straight over the mountains so fast I didn't have time to think. It was a peaceful, quiet day; and all of a sudden…it was unexpected…we didn't wake up knowing bombs would be dropping out of the sky over our heads. We didn't know. That's where it all started.

The belly of the plane began to open. Straight down the middle it parted. And then, well, I think you could guess what happened next. The bombs came. Straight from the middle of the huge, metal planes' bellies, the bombs came; and like instinct, we ran for the caves.

The caves were around our area, in the highlands, the mountains. They were our "storm cellars". In 1944 we were there a lot. They kept us safe when the Americans would bomb the Germans. See, the Americans thought they were doing good by bombing them, but people never think about everyone else who lives there. They don't think about the collateral damage they're creating.

We sat in there, Bastiano and I, and some of our other neighbors awhile. My mother and my sister were there too. We saw the bombs falling from the sky. We watched them explode and disperse every which way. We hid, and we waited, and we hid, until the coast was clear.

Bastiano went home with his family, and I with mine. Although soon after this incident I don't know if I would have called it home. We didn't have any say over our property anymore. We didn't have many resources anymore. We were outcasts in our own land, and the Germans were our owners.

We walked through our door one day, and there, pacing our kitchen floor, in his gray-green uniform, was a German soldier. I couldn't understand him. He spoke German. I had only known Italian at the time, but I was able to gather he needed to collect goods. When he ordered, we listened. We'd get in a heap of trouble if we didn't. Those Germans, they didn't put up with anything. They weren't very pleasant either.

***

It was in the beginning of 1944 when the Germans came and all of the voyages out of Italy were canceled. Before their intrusion on our small, hilltop town, we lived in peace.

I grew up in Ripi, in the province of Frosinone, Italy. It was farm country full of olives and grapes, nothing elaborate, but it was home.

I was only nine months old when my father left for America, just like many other Italians did at that time—to work to provide a better life for us. So, growing up it was just my mother, myself, and my sister, Lina. Just the three of us and a large piece of land to take care of. We were workers, even at the young age of six, I was a worker. We had to maintain and grow our own crops and livestock. It wasn't easy, but we were self-sufficient. We ate and lived off the land.

In Italy, we never laid around. We played a little bit with the kids around, ya know, but nothing to talk about. Most of the time I was doing chores. Me and my sister, Lina, had to participate, we had to help out. In the mornings I used to go out, take care of the animals, milk the cow, feed the animals. Then I would go to school, come home, and before I did any homework I would go back out and take care of the animals. It was a daily routine. Peaceful.

*

A visual of the little town on a hill—Ripi, Frosinone, Italy

2.

Maybe thirty, forty miles from my house sat Monte Cassino, a monastery on the top of a mountain, where it was said the Germans were taking hold during the war. Back and forth everyday the Germans went, using my house, and the houses throughout our town, as their quarters. Nobody really knew what they were doing up at Monte Cassino, but they took everything, whatever they could find—livestock, dry goods. Everything. You couldn't say no. We hid stuff from them—we had to; otherwise we would have had absolutely nothing. We used to dig a hole in the back of the dark wine cellar and fill it with a barrel of food and goods—whatever we had—and covered it up. That's how we preserved it. It was survival of the fittest. You couldn't say no to the Germans. You just couldn't.

As a young boy, I saw many things as the convoys, soldiers, Germans, and people of all different countries and races walked on the big, open road to Monte Cassino. I knew most of them were Polish and Moroccan, but I didn't know why they were foraging on or where they were foraging to. All I knew is that they were going somewhere.

I used to stand on the high, open area of the terrain around my house and watch them all walk by. I saw things—terrible things. I saw things a young boy probably shouldn't see—the horrifying treatment of women, children, and people in general. They were vicious. It wasn't right. This was during the time that Mussolini signed on as allies with Hitler—and Hitler, well, he wanted to take over Europe, and any country he went through, he was doing anything he had to do in order to occupy it.

***

Our neighbors started getting frustrated with the German soldiers. They couldn't take it anymore—the abuse, the constant taking of goods and services, and the treatment that was just so inhumane. They couldn't stand being bossed around in their own home, on their own land. One day they retaliated. And on that day, and it was unfortunate, but one of the Germans…they, well, they got killed. The next day the German Generals and Majors went around from house to house investigating. They wanted to know who had killed one of their soldiers. Of course nobody stood up and said, "I did it", because they didn't want to get in trouble. And so the Germans took the heads of our homes—about a dozen of them, sons and fathers—and brought them to the fields back behind our houses. The Germans ordered the twelve men to dig a trench, and after, lined them up side by side. Shots were fired at the row of men taken from their homes and all of them were buried when they were through; it didn't matter to the Germans that some were only wounded and still alive, they were buried anyway.

My neighbors were some of those twelve men. The Germans slaughtered my neighbors. It was a sad time. I saw it all happen, I heard it all happen. And everyone, all the people around town, they were talking about it. The Germans destroyed my neighbors. They destroyed them—scarring the entire town in the process. You couldn't say no to these people, they didn't want to listen.

***

As horrible as the Germans were to many of my people, strangely, they took a liking towards me. I think it had to do with my name—Italo. They associated it with Hitler. They treated me well. Some nights some of them sat with us around the fireplace and tried to talk with us. After awhile I picked up a few words, but mostly we couldn't understand them. You could tell some of them were nice people, family people. They would show us pictures of their wives and kids. It makes you think. These men, out in battle… and God forbid they get killed…what do they have then? Nothing. What do their families have then? Loss. That's what's bad about wars. People have to understand that. It's not the leaders behind the desk that get hurt, no. It's all the innocent people, young people, family people, that go out on this battlefield and fight—ducking from bullets, dodging all of that; some never being able to come home. When is enough, enough? When the world is nothing but a graveyard?

It's never easy in war. It's not an easy thing, ya know, when you have to fight for your life.

3.

One night I was sleeping in my bed when I heard the sound again—that horrible, familiar sound that meant planes were coming. It woke me up, that sound. And we started running again. My house was too close to Monte Cassino—the mountain the sacred monastery sat on. It was too close to what the Americans thought was a German observational base. Once those Americans got the "OK" to bomb it, we were running for the caves in our surrounding mountains more often than not. That's all we did—hear the boom of the planes… run. During the day… run. That's all we used to do… run.

One day, I remember, we were standing around outside when the bombs started falling. We were safe, for the most part, from the actual explosion, but we weren't safe from the metal that used to fly off of the bombs when they deployed. We called that metal shrapnel. Anyway, it so happened that this shrapnel came down that night and took one of my uncle's shoelaces right off. Could you believe? It took his shoelaces? Thank God that's all it took from him. Many of times that shrapnel has taken worse.

Bastiano got it bad one night. That shrapnel came down and side swiped him. His whole side opened and gushed blood. We had to rush him to the hospital that night. I thank God he made it through too. In conditions like these you get in the habit of thanking God everyday that you, your family, and your friends, were still alive.

Our home lives became more peaceful toward the end of the war, when the Americans came. That's when the Germans fled our area. They didn't want to get stuck there with the Americans. They didn't want to lose their lives. Everyone in Ripi was overjoyed. We didn't have to worry about the harassment from those Germans anymore. Of course, we couldn't understand the Americans either—we couldn't understand English. They were more pleasant, though. They tried to give us things to survive.

Although they brought good with them, there was some bad to the Americans too. They weren't violent like the Germans, no, but their attitudes weren't all that pleasant. Very arrogant they were. No matter what nationality, you've got the good and the bad.

At this point, when the Americans came, it was thought that the Germans were all up on the top of the mountain by Monte Cassino. The Americans were like sitting ducks. They had no way to get up the mountain. Unfortunately, a lot of people got killed that way. Like I said before though, the Americans got the signal that they were allowed to bomb the monastery, and so they did. They bombed the holy ground, only to find that there was nothing to be had. The Germans weren't occupying it. The Americans torched it for no reason at all. All that killing, all that bombing, all that time…wasted.

4.

Once the beginning of 1945 rolled around, the war was over in our area and everything went back to normal again. We didn't have to hide anything from the soldiers anymore and we didn't have to give up our land to the soldiers anymore. I was also able to go back to school again. During the war, we tried to have school in a small, local church that wasn't really in use at the time because we didn't have any priests. After awhile, though, they shut the school down and I couldn't go to school at all during the wartime.

At the time the war ended I was about nine years old and fell back into my old routine again—I worked the fields in the morning, went to school, came back, did homework, and took care of the animals and their feeding and maintenance. It felt good to have a sense of routine again and to have to work again. As a kid, that's all I did was work. It was all I knew.

My mother was a hard worker, too. She and the workers she hired worked all day out in the fields. They'd eat breakfast out in the field and they'd eat lunch out in the field, but they'd always go home for dinner. Bringing food and drinks out to her and the workers during the day was also a job of mine. I liked helping out.

In the fields they'd make sure the crops were good, they'd plant seed, watch the crops grow, of course, then harvest the crops when they were ready, and start all over again in the Fall. It was a nice little system we had. It worked out well. It's how we survived.

On Sundays, my mother would go into the city in Ripi—leaving my sister and I to prepare the dinner. Lina did the cooking and I slaughtered the chicken. At nine years old I'd take the chicken, lay it right on the table, and slaughter it. I felt proud to do that for my family. I had to make sure we survived.

***

It's true, before it was peaceful again, the Germans instilled a fear in me—in everyone they came into contact with—but it was my uncle I was most afraid of in those days, and the days after the war. He didn't wear a uniform like the soldiers, but he was just like a Gustapo—a tough man in charge, watching you everywhere you went, every time you made a move.

Our land was connected, you see. His and ours. There was four quadrants of land—we each had two. But to get to the furthest quadrant of land that was ours, we had to cross over a little piece of community property. Lina and I used to walk down to that back piece, and cross over our shared land—his eyes watching us the entire time.

He was a sick man. He wanted our property, and he did everything in his power to make that known—even if it meant threatening his family. One time, he took his grandson, Vincenzo, and together they laid down in the community land so that no one was able to cross with livestock. He was an arrogant man, so full of himself. We couldn't take his ways any longer.

We tried to sell our land—and people were interested, but when they saw what and who they would have to deal with if they bought it, they quickly backed out. We were left with no choice. We had to sell it to my uncle. Of course, then, he went around bragging about how cheap he got it from us.

My mother threw a little curse at his whole family. Within a whole year that entire family was gone. No joke. Dead. My uncle's son and daughter, both around 45 years old, and my uncle and aunt, both within a week of each other…dead.

My father had four brothers. Two of them, and himself, moved out of the area because of my uncle. Nobody ever got along with him.

***

A few years went by after the war, and again, we received a letter from my father full of legal documents. He was calling us to America for a second time. This time, nothing—no battles, no war—stood in our way.

I had to say goodbye to my cousins and my friend, Bastiano. It was a hard thing to do—part from the people you grew up with, spent so much time with, and saw such horrible things with—but I knew I'd see them again one day… and I was right. I've been back to Italy to visit and Bastiano actually doesn't live too far from me nowadays. Right in White Plains, NY he lives. Goodbye isn't forever.

5.

February 28, 1947 we began our voyage across the Atlantic Ocean on the Saturnia, which was the name of our ship. The ships back then were much smaller than the ones we have today. It wasn't a Carnival cruise ship, that's for sure.

The Saturnia looked somewhat like a battleship. I guess it was the way the ship was shaped and what our sleeping quarters looked like that make me remember it that way. We all slept in a big, long room filled with bunk beds. There weren't any separate compartment rooms for people to sleep in like there is today. It wasn't a cruise ship. It was tough. It was very tough the way we grew up.

I remember the waters were rough. In the pajamas my mother made for me before we left Italy, I used to walk up to the top deck of the ship, stand in the doorway looking out at the ocean, and watch the waves go over the ship from side to side. I didn't want to just hang around in the cabin below, so I went up to the top to see what was out there. Of course there was nothing out there anyway. We were the only ship to be seen, surrounded by black, dark waters. I remember saying to myself, "There's nobody out here. What are we doing out here?" It was very strange to me—I had never been out on the ocean like that before. I remember I just kept thinking, we're all alone out on the seas here… God forbid… where would we go? I wasn't a swimmer, that's for sure. I don't know what I would have done.

My mother, sister, and some bunkmates used to get seasick down below. They made me their cabin boy—I would always go up to the kitchen and bring them food, in my pajamas of course. I really loved those pajamas. They were so comfortable that I didn't take them off the entire twelve days it took us to sail to America. Could you believe it took twelve days? Nowadays it takes only nine hours by plane. It was different times.

I still remember the morning we got to New York. It was March the 12th. We were the first ship that didn't have to go through Ellis Island. Instead we went through this other pier. It was somewhere around 42nd Street.

I recognized a man waving to us as we pulled into the pier. His face was the first thing I saw. Even though I hadn't seen it since I was nine months old, I knew right away… he had that look. That was the Recine face. That was the first time I met my father.

***

I was born in 1936. Like I've said, nine months after that, my father left for America. He wanted to do the right thing, he wanted to make a better life and then bring the family over. If it weren't for the war, we would probably have been to America sooner, but unfortunately you don't always have control over everything happening around you.

Growing up, I knew I had a father, but there's things I missed when he wasn't around. Communication was hard, especially during the war, so we didn't even hear from him too often. To see him for the first time, well, it felt good. It's hard to explain, though. The first time you meet your father after what, 11 years? When you're just nine months old you don't really have any memories or anything. I had really nothing to go on... but I knew once I saw that face of the man waving to us, that he was my father. It was an incredible feeling. I just knew.

*

My sister, Lina, and I aboard the Saturnia on our 12-day journey to
America, dressed in the pajamas my mother made for me

A family portrait—myself, my father, mother, and sisters, Maria, the younger one, and Lina, the older one

6.

We were a family of workers introduced to the opportunities of America, so it was no surprise that we were able to buy a house within our first year living here. Everybody pitched in, everybody worked, and we made it happen… 97 Brisbin Street, Jamaica, Queens. It was ours.

It was a big, two-family house that we had. It was us living in there and some boarders my mother took on to supplement the income. Money wasn't as good, but it was sufficient enough to support our household. That's all that mattered. The boarders were good. They paid their fees, took care of their needs, and weren't much of a bother. They really just helped us out.

While we tried our best to merge with the American culture, it wasn't always that easy. The language, especially, was a huge barrier—I had to repeat the third grade because of it. When I was in Italy, I had passed the third grade. When I came here, though, they thought it would be best to hold me back while I started to learn English. It didn't set me back much. I continued to work hard, and I made it through.

By the age of twelve I started working—just a little after we first came to America. I had to bring money home, you know, that's how we survived—we all did our part. During the week, after school, I would work at the Italian Deli and on the weekend I worked at the theater. I had two jobs growing up—I had to; the money wasn't like what it is today, it was very little. Working at the movie theater I made 25 cents an hour. That's big bucks, don't ya think? That's why I needed the Deli job, too. Between that and the theater, my sister doing her part, and my father taking on construction work, we survived. We struggled, but we survived.

***

Growing up I didn't have much time for play. I wanted to, sure, and did a little bit in the neighborhood, but I knew I needed to work to help out the family, so I couldn't participate much. I really loved baseball. In fact, I tried out for the high school team because I liked it so much. What's more, is that I was pretty good at it too. I used to be a power hitter. Man, I could hit, and I was fast—not that I want to brag about it.

The whole time I was trying out, I knew I wasn't cut out to play on the team, though. Sure, I had the abilities, but the way I was raised I was taught there wasn't any time for play. It was all work, all the time. Even when I would play in the neighborhood once and a while I knew my family didn't enjoy me going out. So when I asked them if I could play baseball on the high school team, I wasn't surprised when they told me no. "No, you gotta go to work" they said, "Baseball is play. You're not supposed to play. You gotta go to work." What could I do? I couldn't disobey them, so I went to work.

I was held back a lot growing up, and I wish I had played baseball for that team. I was really into it, and I was good. I mean who knows, I might've made the pros. I remember seeing my friends going out and playing on the high school teams. I was jealous, I wanted to be with them playing on those teams. I missed out. I honestly missed out a lot on just going out and having some fun, participating in the things I enjoyed. But what can you do? That's what life was. You have to accept it and make the best of it. That's all.

Me on the stoop of our house: 97 Brisbin Street, Jamaica, Queens, NY

7.

My high school years were full of studies, work, and Anita. I was a senior when I met her at Woodrow Wilson High School, near where she was from. We met through acquaintances. Me and a group of my friends used to hang out around a candy shop on Rockaway Boulevard in South Ozone Park before school started. I was a big shot at the time because I had a car—a 1954 Chevy. I was the King Pin, ya know—like Elvis Presley (I didn't wear any peg pants like him though). Anyway, Anita started hanging around us in the mornings and that's how we met.

Every morning we used to take a ride around the neighborhood before classes started. I used to drop my friends off at school first and then ride around for a half hour with Anita. It was beautiful. I joke around and say she only liked me for my car, but even now, as I'm telling this story, she's yelling, "I did not just like you for your car!" I guess we'll have to take her word for it. Anyway, we started seeing each other after awhile and would go out together. It was hard for us to get together sometimes though, because I was busy working and she was busy working, too.

Anita lost her father when she was young. It was only Anita, her sister, Linda, her brother, Jack, and her mother. They were the only ones left, and they had to take care of the home. It was tough for her, too, so free weekends were pretty hard to come by for us; but we went to each other's proms and started dating steadier after that.

I remember one day we were sitting at the candy store when one of my buddies whispered, "You should take her to the prom" while pointing at Anita. Of course I already knew I wanted to take her to my prom. There was just one little battle I had to overcome first.

My parents were very strict. They didn't really allow me to have fun. That's what it was in those days; so, I had to sneak out to go to the prom. Before dinner, I put my nice dress clothes on, and then on top of them I put on old, regular clothes. After dinner, I sneaked upstairs, took my top layer of clothes off, and snuck out of the house. I made it to Anita's and to the prom without anybody stopping me. That was our first date. I did the same thing again when I took Anita to her prom. My parents were so set in their ways. It had a lot to do with the fact that Anita was American. An Italian dating an American wasn't as accepted as it is today. It was a struggle, but we made it—to our proms, and in life.

I had to sneak out of the house almost every weekend. We went to a variety of movies and shows together,

Anita and I. I'm not much of a dancer, so we didn't do much dancing. Sometimes we went to a party or a wedding—all family affairs. There wasn't much nightclubbing going on in those days like there is today, so we didn't do much of that, but we had fun. We liked spending time together.

***

In 1955 it came time for me to graduate from high school. From there I went into the family business… construction. My father was always in the construction line and when it came time for me to work full time, I couldn't say no to him. So, into construction I went.

I was making $2.00 an hour working construction at my father's company. After awhile I got the nerve to ask my father and his partners for a raise. I was doing a bunch of things for them, working for everybody—driving the truck, doing the surveying, setting the forms, working in carpentry, and moving material from job to job all by myself. I never wanted any help because I thought that would be time wasted, I figured I was saving him money by doing that. I deserved a raise, and they gave me just that. Instead of $2.00 an hour, I was making $2.10 an hour. What a big jump that was, right? Some big money that was.

It was good, though. I can laugh about it today.

I had no problem working with my father in the construction line. I learned a lot, I did a lot. By doing, you learn. That's important, never stop doing, never stop learning, because then what do you have?

***

Anita stuck with me after my graduation and throughout my construction jobs. After about four years of going steady with her I said, "Well that's enough all ready." One day we met a jeweler, bought a ring, and what did ya know, we were engaged. I thought it was about time we got married. On November 16 of 1958 we were wed… despite my parent's disapproval.

They didn't come to the wedding, my parents that is. They didn't accept the fact that I was marrying an American girl of Irish and Spanish decent. In their eyes if she wasn't Italian, I shouldn't be marrying her. But I did anyway. Anita was worth it.

We had our ceremony at Queens Terrace—a catering hall where all the young brides used to go to get married. It was a nice, small wedding. In those days you didn't go big because there wasn't any money. Not much of my family came. The only one that did was my brother-in-law, Filippo. Not even my sister, Lina, came—she had a young baby at home to take care of. I felt let down, lonely, abandoned—somewhat of a loner. Of course I was overjoyed to be marrying the love of my life, but my family not being there to support me… well that hurt.

We honeymooned in Niagra Falls in Canada. We drove up there, Anita and I, with no plans, just an idea.

We shot from the hips. I had family in Montreal so we wound up visiting them and staying with some family in Watertown, NY on our way back. We didn't spend much time up there because we couldn't really afford to take too much time off. I was lucky to get that little bit of time off as it was. It was November—the end of the season. We were working hard to get stuff done before they closed jobs down for the spring. But I got the time, so we took a little trip, and that was it. Simple.

Eleven months later I was drafted into the service. I spent my first anniversary in a boot camp for basic training in Fort Hood, Texas. It was called "Hell on Wheels". It was the armored tank division. Don't you think that was nice? Spending my first anniversary in a place like that?

It was no fun. It was no fun at all.

I kind of wound up with the short end of the stick actually. It was the law back then that if you were twenty-four years or older you couldn't be drafted. I was just a few months short of twenty-four when they called me in. Pretty bad luck, huh?

I have to thank God, though. After my first and second phase of training, at Fort Leonardwood, Missouri, Anita came with me and we stayed together, living off post in Missouri—the two of us. I took up heavy equipment engineering there. That's where I learned my trade.

It turned out to be a good experience. I had never left my home in New York until the day I was drafted. I was always home. Anita was always home. We didn't go too many places because we didn't have the money. Money wasn't as abundant as it is today. I'm glad I had that experience, though—even if I was living in the middle of Missouri, on a tight budget in the service. I was able to see new places and experience new things. You learn that way. You grow.

The night of our engagement

Anita and I on our wedding day

8.

Life in the service was nice. It wasn't all that bad. We had many friends and barely any money at all. We were poorer than poor. We played cards. Oh, we played a lot of cards… for beans because nobody had money at all. Sixty dollars a month—that's all we used to live on. Could you believe just sixty dollars a month? That would be impossible today. Of course we had to pay rent with some of that sixty dollars, too. It wasn't a picnic.

Usually when you get drafted, you don't get much of a choice about where you're going to work, but once I found out they needed me, I put in for working with heavy equipment. I was fortunate enough that they gave it to me. This was during peacetime.

I was an engineer, so to speak—a heavy equipment combat engineer. I used to travel because of that. In the summertime we went from Missouri to Wisconsin to train the National Guard and the new reserves on how to build bridges, roads, maintain and run the equipment… all of that. In the winter and fall months we would travel back to Missouri again and do basically the same routine there and go out and take care of the roads.

I used to go out with the A, B, and C Companies too. They had to do some work, so they called us, and we'd go out with the equipment and do the work for them. That's how I learned to operate the machinery. I used to teach the other men how to run the equipment while I was in the service, because they wanted to learn too. It was a give and take experience. I learned something new everyday.

It was nothing to talk about, living off post, but you did what you had to do. It was good sometimes because we lived in the same compound as our friends and we would have get-togethers that were nice. There's good and bad to everything.

*

Me, operating some heavy machinery during my time in the service

Anita and I during my time in the service

***

In 1961 I was supposed to get out of the service, my time was supposed to be done. Of course, though, you can't control the world around you—issues in the Cold War and Berlin began, and John F. Kennedy extended my service six more months. This was another little battle we had to deal with.

One day we got the orders that we were going to get shipped out to Berlin. Anita was pregnant with our first child at the time, and so we planned for her to go back home to Queens while I was overseas. We were fortunate though… just a few days before we were about to leave, President John F. Kennedy informed us we weren't needed in Germany anymore—the world was still peaceful. It worked out well for us. Who knows how long I would've been there for?

We stayed out my remaining time in the service in Missouri, where we welcomed our daughter, also named Anita, on October 28.

In 1962 they finally let me out of the service and so my new family and I went home to Queens, New York. I went straight to work doing construction. I was a union operator making nice money.

***

It was after my time in the service that my relationship with my parents started to get better. I think a lot of that had to do with the fact that they then had a grandchild. We used to visit them more and they finally started to feel more comfortable and warmer toward us. I thank God for that. There's certain things you miss when your parents aren't around as often.

9.

Anita and I, we saved money all of the time. That was important to us. Even while I was in the service, we saved money. I know that's hard to believe because we didn't get the kind of money in the service where it was easy to save, but we did it, we needed to. We saved money from the job I had when we got back from Missouri, too, and with all our savings we were able to buy our first house on Long Island—brand new… 117 Ledgewood Drive, Smithtown, NY. We moved in just two weeks before Christmas, December 15, 1962.

I was happy we were able to buy this house. It was in a good area, near good schools—all important things for a young family. In 1965 our family got bigger with the birth of our son, Ricardo; and in 1967 it got even bigger with the birth of our other son, Michael. It was a blessing to have three, beautiful children. I am very happy and proud to call them mine. They're good kids—even growing up they were good kids. Sure, sometimes they got out of hand, fought with each other, and did the wrong thing, but I was still, and I am still, proud of them. There's good blood in them.

***

After we moved into our house on Ledgewood, I was working with a big company, called Portier and McClain, and landed a big road job in the city—in the Bronx area. We did a whole stretch of road on that job. The road is called the Major Sheridan Expressway nowadays. Pretty cool, right? That's when I was operating the road grader. I used to grade the road base before we installed the concrete which would give the roadway a finish. I worked with that big company for about a year.

When that job ended another one came about I was working with a builder that built Diners. I got a job as a handyman, with the experience I got working with my father in construction. It came very easy for me to do anything that had to be done. After I worked with this new boss for a while he saw what I was able to do. He got to liking me. I always told him that I always liked to operate heavy construction equipment. Then he told me that he had a personal friend that had a heavy construction equipment business in Flushing, Queens and that he was going to recommend me to them. Charles Lobosco & Son the company was called. When I got there, the first thing they asked me was, "what was I able to do?" I said, "everything" and told them of all the experience I had operating all the different types of equipment. Then I was hired. Just like that.

Later on the builder that recommended me for this construction job told me that if at any time I needed a job, there would be an opening for me with him. Hearing that, well, that made me feel very good—knowing I was wanted for the things I could do. Back in the 60's I worked with him during the winter months doing interior diner building. In the spring, I would go back to Charles Lobosco & Son operating heavy equipment, just as I liked to do. I did this for about 2 years until work started to slow down. Then another job came about. Another job always came about.

Soon after I was working with another heavy equipment company. This company was called Guarino Brothers. It leased out different machinery, along with its operator, to different contractors. If someone needed a job done, they'd call my boss and he'd get me to go out and do it. I did whatever they needed me to do. I liked to work.

Work, work, work. That's all I ever did, was work, work, work. I never stopped. I never wanted to have to go out with my hands open. I wanted to be self-sufficient and provide the best for my family. I didn't want any handouts. I still don't.

After business with the Guarino Brothers started to slow down, I decided to go into my own business with a partner, who, unfortunately, became difficult to work with. Ledgewood Paving Corp was its name. We paved with concrete and asphalt.

I ran my own equipment. I had a road grader, the rollers and the spreaders, and I would do a lot of the work by myself to keep the cost down. Of course we had a crew to do some work too, I couldn't do it all on my own. Business was good in the beginning for us. We lasted ten years working with pavement and concrete, but after awhile it started slowing down for us, and honestly, I couldn't stand working with my partner for much longer. That's when we began thinking about what would come next.

We had hardly any money at the time, Anita and I, but together we decided to start our own business. We went into private sanitation. Anita ran the office and I ran the fields—doing the work and maintenance to keep our little business going. We couldn't afford to pay many people to help us out at the time, so for then it was just her and I… oh and Mr. Willy—the one helper we could afford. Me and Mr. Willy used to drive the one truck we owned. I thank God that everything eventually started to blossom for us. We called it ARMAR Carting Corp.

ARMAR is an interesting name isn't it? Well, each letter stands for each person in our little family. Anita, Ricardo, Michael, Anita, and Ray—which, I didn't mention earlier, was the name they used to call me in the service. We called each other by our last names and all my pals shortened Recine to Ray. I figured I liked it well enough, and what did ya know, it stuck. So I kept it.

It became very well established, our business. It became very well known, and a good business people profited by. It was tough getting there, but we worked hard, and we did it.

*

'59 Ford—our first car together

My work on the back of the house on Ledgewood Drive in Smithtown, NY

The front of the Ledgewood house

At the door of our garbage business, ARMAR Carting

10.

It had always been a dream of mine to build my own home. My whole life I wanted to do it. I liked the idea of starting from nothing and building something beautiful—something worth living in. I liked the adventure it created and the progress I was able to see. Of course, Anita didn't want to move and start over. She was perfectly happy where we were. She thought I was crazy—especially after all the work we put into the house on Ledgewood. Yeah, she was annoyed with me for a while.

We were a team, though, and she wound up supporting me. The business was established and we had a bit of money, so I figured now was as good a time as any to start work on this dream of mine. We found a nice piece of property in Head of the Harbor, NY—it took us five years to pay it off. After those five years, we got the permits to build the house. The year was 1980 that we started, what I like to call, our "family project". Of course our kids didn't really want to work and help out, but they did—working hard is how you get ahead in life.

This project didn't come easily and it took time—about two years. For two years, nobody went anywhere. After work I used to go to the site and build, on weekends too. Anita and the kids always wanted to go to the beach. There was no time. No time for the beach, I told them. We had to work… we all had to work. I think we went to the beach once in awhile, not often, but once in a while. Anita would like it to be known that we never once went to that beach. I can laugh about it today. What could I do? We had a job to do, and look where we are now.

I was lucky I had the support of my family and the help of some friends in the construction business. I did all the grading and the excavation. I cleared the property, too. We did the footing on the house and some buddies of mine helped out with the bigger work. A friend of mine helped me and Anita pour the concrete, another friend helped me frame the whole house, another did all the electrical work for me, and a few others did the insulation, sheet rock, and Spackle. It's a great thing, in life, to have people who are willing to help you out. It's all about giving and receiving. I'd do the same thing for them. It's important to have relationships like that in your life.

After all that major stuff was done, Anita and my daughter painted the whole house. Me and the boys did all the exterior work. Two years it took. Could you believe? Two years to get that house into move-in condition. I thank God everyday for the help I had. You can't build anything in life, or get anywhere, without the help and support of others.

*

The house we built

11.

My whole life I did a lot of work—a little bit of everything. Whatever I had to do, I did it. I didn't back off from it, no sir. As a matter of fact, I enjoyed doing the work because I liked to learn. I used to absorb everything. I used to watch people do the work and then say, "Alright now let me try it". You learn something, put it aside; learn the trade, put it aside; always keep it in mind. You never know when you're going to need it. Ya never know when it'll come in handy. Become versatile that way.

Get out there, don't be afraid, insert yourself.

I worked with everything, from carpentry to equipment to concrete, blocks and asphalt. I can do anything today if I want to do it; because I put my mind to doing it; because I have done it; because I knew one day I was going to use it. Now that I've got my own home, I do it all. I don't have to call anybody to do anything for me.

Get out there, don't be afraid, insert yourself.

With work, though, comes sacrifice. I was traveling all the time, I was never home. It was hard, but I had to make a living for my family. That was life.

It was the worst when I was traveling back and forth into Manhattan. I used to go work there six out of the seven days of the week—sometimes I even worked seven days. I left in the dark and came home in the dark. I never saw my kids—they were always sleeping when I left, and they were always sleeping when I came home. What type of business was that? I missed out on a lot. I missed them growing up. No good. I missed that. It's no good. I think about this everyday. You have to stay with the family. It's the most important thing.

It was nicer when I established myself out on Long Island. The job itself wasn't easier, but it was closer to home. I had more of a home life. That was more important.0

***

Anita and I always worked as a team. We both worked very hard. I did all the work outside—bringing the money home for the family to live on. She did all the work inside—working the office for me and taking care of the kids growing up. That was theory back then, to have a stay-at-home mom. That's how it used to be in those days. The best thing in life is to have support amongst the whole family.

I idolize my family. You can't go wrong when you put family first, you can only go ahead. You'll have a good life that way.

12.

Since leaving Italy as a young boy, I've been back a few times. I enjoy it every time I go. It's my roots. The lifestyle growing up there is much different now as opposed to when I was growing up. Life has changed one hundred percent. Today, it's all up-to-date. It was much more laid back in my day; we didn't have all that flashy technology stuff. It wasn't easy, but thank God we survived. Through the drive and the willpower, you'll make it.

We were hard workers in Italy. My whole family was hard workers—must be the Recine trait. That's how you get ahead in life. You do have to have the fun, but you also have to have the mind to work hard. If you don't have any money, you don't have any fun. Everything goes hand in hand.

When I lived in Italy, there were three houses all attached. One house was for my Uncle, my father's brother, one house was for my father's second cousins, and one house was for us. That's how the family stayed close. Now, they go their separate ways, they have their own individual homes. I guess that's just modern times.

It was a nice tradition that we had over there in Italy. It was more home life and togetherness. Here in America, you have family all over the country. It's no fun that way. Family is very important to me. You have to be a little bit family oriented. It's the best bet.

I miss it now because my people are still there. I want to go back and see how they're doing, I want to stay in touch. It's very important. They're good people, my cousins. They'll welcome you with open arms. They can't do enough for you. That's how good of people they are. Their door is always open—that's how it's supposed to be. In Italy, the family unit is very close knit, they all live in the same house. That's just how it is, well, at least that's how it's always been. The wife used to move into the husband's childhood home and live with his family. Nowadays I think the tradition has changed.

When I go back to Italy now, I feel very warm when I'm there—no, not just because of the weather. Sometimes I feel like I'm missing out, being in America. I miss my family that I have there especially. I'm getting older, and so are they. There's no good feelings when I think about that. We grew up together, we went through so much together, and I miss being around them. They're family.

The closest cousin that I have in Italy is Dominick—the rest, unfortunately, have passed on. We used to yell to each other out on the verandas of our house back all those years ago—especially when we were trying to do homework. One would ask the question and the other would try and give him an answer. We didn't have any cell phones in those days. We didn't need them—the sound carried over there through the valleys just fine.

When I left Italy, I was so young that I missed out on a lot of my cousin Dominick's milestones—just like he missed out on a lot of mine. I wasn't there for his wedding or any of his kids being born—nothing like that. When I go back now, I see how much time has passed. I see how much I've missed. It's not a good feeling.

I think about Dominick all the time, I do. I'm always thinking about him. Now that I'm older, I feel like I'm even further away from him, and I don't want to be. I want to get closer to him. I hope everything works out for him.

***

The first time I went back to Italy since being in America was back in 1956, after I graduated high school. I went with my mother, father, and sisters. We visited all of our family that was living there at the time. This was also the time when my mother tried to marry me off to an Italian girl. She knew I was going with Anita at the time, but she didn't like the fact that I was dating an American girl—an Irish/Spanish American girl, no less. Her sneaky agenda didn't work, though. I came back to Anita fully, with no Italian girl hanging onto me at all.

I went back again around 1967 with Anita to take care of some business with our property. We rented a car while we there, for a whole week, and we did a drive around the country. We drove the whole east coast, spent a day in Venice, then came around and drove the west coast. It was nice, we drove a lot but we saw a lot. It was a good adventure.

When I was a kid we never went anywhere. I never saw any part of Italy other than Ripi before this trip. I never saw anything past my home in America and my post in the service. I didn't have the opportunity to travel the world at eighteen like many of the kids get to do today. Sure, I would've liked to, but what're you going to do? I just have to enjoy it now.

We went back again another time and my cousin took us around. We went to Pompeii, Pisa, Naples, Capri, Amalfi, Rome. It was all very nice. I'm glad I was able to see the places I've always wanted to see. There's one place I look forward to the most, though, and that's my hometown. Ripi—a small town, a farm town; not quite the same as Manhattan. You have to be able to appreciate what they have. They may not have a lot, but to me, it sure is something. In Ripi—at home—all you do is eat, drink, and laugh. It's all you need.

We actually went back again with my daughter and her kids. We did some sightseeing in different parts of the country and ended our trip in Ripi. I was very glad to see them meet the rest of our family. They were able to see where their roots came from; I think that's very important. I was very proud to have them with me there. I want to take the rest of my family there, too, one day. I'd like them to see where they come from.

Yeah, we've gone back quite a couple times. I just can't stay away.

My cousin, Don Roberto, the priest who took me and Anita on a trip around Italy

A photo of what my house in Ripi looks like now

During another trip to visit home, Me, Anita and my cousin, Domenico and his wife, Anna

A photo taken during one of my visits back in my hometown. From left to right: Caterina, Luigino and his wife, Domenico and his wife, Anna, me, Anita, Peter and his wife, Lucia

13.

Now, of course, I'm retired—Anita and I live in a small senior development in Lake Grove, NY. My son, Michael, and his family live in the house we built. I thank God he's living there. He appreciates it.

When I first retired, I thought that I was going to miss working. I actually thought I was never going to retire at all because I never wanted to. I'm a workaholic. I don't know what possessed me to actually do it—retire, I mean. I turned 65 one day and decided that was it. I was done. I've worked since I was 12 years old; I've never lost a day of work. I guess when I decided to retire, I thought, now is my time. I didn't enjoy life when I was younger, so I wanted to enjoy it now.

It was hard, of course, letting go of the business. Luckily our boys—Rick and Mike—were working there and wanted to stay on… so we passed the reins over to them and our little family business continued to stay alive. I was happy about that. We have twenty-three trucks running nowadays. We came a long way from when just me and Mr. Willy were running that one truck. I'm very proud of what our family has helped our business grow into.

Now, I'm trying to take it easy, live life a little. I'm trying to make up for what I lost when I was younger. I worked hard sure, and I survived, but I couldn't do anything and I couldn't go anywhere because of the work. Work, work, work, that's all I ever did.

I want to put a little life into myself. I want to enjoy my life while I still can…because of course I'm not getting any younger. This is where I'm at now; I'm not a kid anymore. I'm trying to stay occupied and active, I don't want to go stale. I don't want to become a vegetable.

I enjoy golfing now, once a week with some buddies of mine, and Anita and I play bocci and shuffleboard at the clubhouse in our complex. We like to travel now, too. We take different river cruises once a year. We've gone on ones through Germany and the Rhine River, Vienna and Amsterdam, France, and Italy. We go to Florida in the winter and spend nice time down there in the warm weather, and we come back up to New York during the spring to spend time with our kids and grandkids. We enjoy all of that. We enjoy spending time with the whole family. Family is very important. When all of us get together, it makes me so proud. I've got a great family. It just… it makes me feel good when I think of everyone together. Family is very important. They are my world.

What I enjoy the most is spending time with them. One of my favorite places to be with everyone is at our little piece of property in upstate, NY. Anita and I bought it back in the mid to late 70s. It was near Scotch Valley, a ski slope where we took our three kids skiing back in the day. They liked to ski, and were pretty good at it, too. I tried skiing only once, but I didn't really take to it, so I gave it up. Anita skied for a while until her leg gave out.

Now, the place is a little different. Most of the nearby slopes are gone and it isn't just our kids that go up to the property with us. Now, our grandkids come, too. Our kids grew up going there and now our grandkids are growing up going there. It's a very special place to me.

It's a big piece of land. We have a nice little house that sits on top of a hill. From the porch you can see the kids playing and riding quads in the fields, heading into the woods to explore in the creek, or fishing on the pond we made—enjoying the fresh air, the nature and the world all around them. It's a nice escape, it is.

There's room up there to do everything. Everyone comes up and spends time together, having the best time. I like to see that. The feeling of love is always there when everyone is together. It's obvious that everyone feels that. You can't pay for that. There's no money value on that. You can't replace it. That place is very special to me. Very special.

*

Me and my kids—Anita, Rick, and Michael—at our upstate house exploring the stream.

My kids and grandkids enjoying their time together at the upstate house

***

My grandkids are good kids. They're aggressive and hustlers. I like what I see in them. They want to get ahead in life, which is good. Maybe that's my blood in them, I don't know. They make me feel proud, though, in everything that they do.

I wish everybody to do well. I want to see that. I want to see everyone do well. I don't want to see anyone struggle. That's why I worked hard to put things together, so my family didn't have to struggle like I did. I made good for the family, so I could raise my family right. That's what I did, or at least that's what I tried to do.

Thank God we are all where we are today, and everyone's doing well—all of my children and grandchildren. They all have their homes and are doing well. Why? Because they worked for it. That's it. Nobody's gonna knock on your door and say, "hello, here it is, here's a gift for you." No. You have to work for it. Everything seems to be working out for them, and I'm happy for that. Sure, they're all going to come across their own battles. But they'll work through it. They're hard workers—all of them. Through the drive and the willpower they'll make it.

*

Afterward

Seventy years in America. That's a long time. Over the years there's some things you remember and some things you forget. Sometimes there's even some things you don't want to remember. There were rough times, but good times, too. Such is life.

Remember the good times, thank the rough times. If there were one thing I would thank the rough times for, it would be for making me realize what could have been, what I have, and why I have strived to get ahead in life. Before I had nothing. Now, I have everything.

Work hard. Love harder. Have the willpower to carry on.

I'd say the big battles are over now. I've worked hard and built a life I'm proud of. It's unfortunate I'm not getting any younger. I figure, though, I might try and enjoy the life that's left.

- Italo Recine

About the Authors

Italo Recine - The proud patriarch revels in the hard work that formed the foundation which allowed his family to flourish here in America. Years later, he is living in a quaint community with his wife, Anita—finally enjoying retirement, although, his wife is always finding him little jobs to do! This story is one he has hoped to pass on to his children, his grandchildren, and generations to come.

Gabrielle Manfredi is the granddaughter of Italo Recine—honored to help bring his life struggles and triumphs to the page in this touching memoir. Gabrielle is currently in graduate school, following in her grandfather's footsteps and working hard, towards her master's degree. Previous published work can be found in the literary collections, 34th Parallel and Arbor Vitae.

Printed in the United States
By Bookmasters